To parents and teachers

We hope you and the children will enjoy reading this story in either English or Spanish. The story is simple, but not *simplified* so the language of the Spanish and the English is quite natural but there is lots of repetition.

At the back of the book is a small picture dictionary with the key words and how to pronounce them. There is also a simple pronunciation guide to the whole story on the last page.

Here are a few suggestions on using the book:

- Read the story aloud in English first, to get to know it. Treat it like any other picture book: look at the pictures, talk about the story and the characters and so on.
- Then look at the picture dictionary and say the Spanish names for the key words. Ask the children to repeat them. Concentrate on speaking the words out loud, rather than reading them.
- Go back and read the story again, this time in English *and* Spanish. Don't worry if your pronunciation isn't quite correct. Just have fun trying it out. Check the guide at the back of the book, if necessary, but you'll soon pick up how to say the Spanish words.
- When you think you and the children are ready, you can try reading the story in Spanish only. Ask the children to say it with you. Only ask them to read it if they are keen to try. The spelling could be confusing and put them off.
- Above all encourage the children to have a go and give lots of praise. Little children are usually quite unselfconscious and this is excellent for building up confidence in a foreign language.

Published by b small publishing ltd
The Book Shed, 36 Leyborne Park, Kew, Richmond, Surrey, TW9 3HA
www.bsmall.co.uk

1 2 3 4 5

Design: *Lone Morton* Editorial: *Catherine Bruzzone* Production: *Madeleine Ehm*
Printed in China by WKT Co. Ltd.
ISBN 978-1-905710-79-9 (paperback with spine)
British Library Cataloguing in Publication Data. A catalogue record for this book is available from the British Library.

Happy birthday!

¡Feliz cumpleaños!

Mary Risk
Pictures by Lucy Keijser
Spanish by Rosa Martín

b small publishing

It's my birthday.

Es mi cumpleaños.

Here are all my friends.
Hi! Hello! Come in, everyone!

Aquí están todos mis amigos.
¡Hola! ¿Qué tal? ¡Entrad todos!

All these presents for me?
What a great mask!

Todos estos regalos para mí?
¡Qué máscara tan estupenda!

And I love this dinosaur!

¡Y me encanta este dinosaurio!

Let's blow some bubbles.
They're huge.

Vamos a hacer pompas de jabón.
¡Son enormes! ¿Verdad?

Whoosh!

four
cuatro

three
tres

five
cinco

two
dos

six
seis

seven
siete

eight
ocho

nine
nueve

ten
diez

¡Ay!

Where have they all gone?

¿Dónde se han ido todas?

Oh! look at Sarah!

¡Ay! ¡Mira a Sara!

Balloons!
Can I have one?

¡Globos!
¿Me das uno?

The red one's for you.
El rojo es para ti.

The green one's for me.
El verde es para mí.

The blue one's for Peter.
El azul es para Pedro.

The purple one's for Clare.
El morado es para Clara.

This is fantastic!
This is fun!

¡Es fantástico!
¡Qué divertido!

Oh dear! Goodbye, balloons!

¡Ay, no! ¡Adiós, globos!

Have you lost your balloon?
Never mind, don't cry!

¿Se te ha escapado el globo?
¡No pasa nada! ¡No llores!

Are you hungry?
Have some cake.

¿Tenéis hambre?
¡Tomad un poco de pastel!

Are you thirsty?
Have a drink.

¿Tienes sed?
Bebe algo.

That was a lovely party.
Thank you for having us.

Ha sido una fiesta muy bonita.
Gracias por invitarnos.

Look! The balloons!

¡Mirad! ¡Los globos!

Goodbye!

¡Adiós!

Pronouncing Spanish

Don't worry if your pronunciation isn't quite correct. The important thing is to be willing to try. The pronunciation guide here is based on the Spanish accent used in Spain. Although it cannot be completely accurate, it certainly will be a great help.

- Read the guide as naturally as possible, as if it were English.
- Put stress on the letters in *italics* e.g. past*el*.

If you can, ask a Spanish speaking person to help and move on as soon as possible to speaking the words without the guide.

Note: Spanish adjectives usually have two forms, one for masculine and one for feminine nouns. They often look very similar but are pronounced slightly differently, e.g., **divertido** and **divertida** (see the word list below).

Words Las palabras

lass pal-*ah*brass

happy birthday!
¡feliz cumpleaños!

fel*eeth* koom-pleh-*an*yoss

cake
el pastel

el pas*tel*

present
el regalo

el reh-*gah*-lo

balloon
el globo
el *glo*-bo

bubble
la pompa de jabón
lah *pom*pa deh hah-*bon*

mask
la máscara
lah *mass*-kah-ra

hi, how are you?
hola, ¿qué tal?
oh-la, keh *tal*

hi/hello
¡hola!
oh-la

thank you
gracias
grah-thee-ass

goodbye
adiós
adee-*oss*

dinosaur
el dinosaurio
el deeno-*zah*-*ow*-reeo

friend
el amigo, la amiga
el ah-*mee*-go/lah ah-*mee*-ga

lovely
bonito/bonita
bo-*nee*-to/bo-*nee*-ta

great
estupendo/estupenda
ess-toop-*en*do/ess-toop-*en*da

fantastic
fantástico/fantástica
fan-*tass*-teeko/fan-*tass*-teeka

fun
divertido/divertida
deevair-*tee*-do/deevair-*tee*-da

party
la fiesta
lah fee*ess*ta

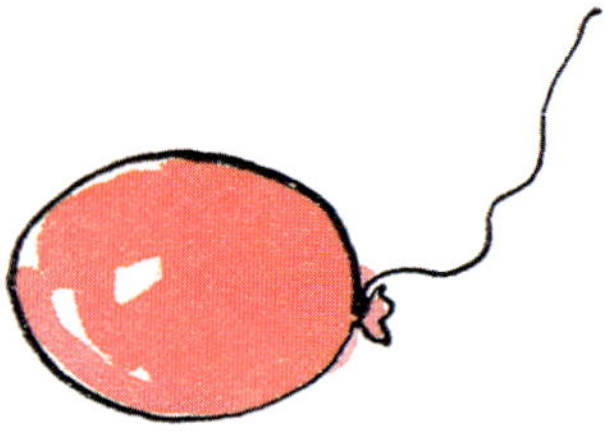

red
rojo/roja
*ro*ho/*ro*ha

purple
morado/a
mo*rah*-do/a

blue
azul
ah*thool*

green
verde
vair-deh

A simple guide to pronouncing this Spanish story

Es mi cumpleaños.
ess mee koom-pleh-*an*yoss

Aquí están todos mis amigos.
a*kee* est*an* toh-doss meess ah-*mee*-goss

¡Hola! ¿Qué tal? ¡Entrad todos!
oh-la, keh tal, entra *toh*-doss

¿Todos estos regalos para mí?
toh-doss estoss reh-*gal*-oss *pah*-ra mee

¡Qué máscara tan estupenda!
keh *mass*-kah-ra tan ess-too-*pen*da

¡Y me encanta este dinosaurio
ee meh en*kan*ta esteh deeno-*zah-ow*-reeo

Vamos a hacer pompas de jabón.
*va*moss ah ath-*air pom*pass deh ha*bon*

¡Son enormes! ¿Verdad?
son eh-*nor*-mess, vair-*da*

una, dos, tres, cuatro, cinco,
seis, siete, ocho, nueve, diez, ¡ay!
*oo*na, doss, trayss, *kwa*tro, *thin*ko, sayss,
see-*eh*teh, *o*cho, noo*eh*beh, dee-*eth,* aye

¿Dónde se han ido todas?
*don*deh seh an eetho *toh*-dass

¡Ay! ¡Mira a Sara!
aye, *mee*ra ah *sah*-ra

¡Globos!
glo-boss

¿Me das uno?
meh dass *oo*no

El rojo es para ti.
el *ro*ho ess *pa*ra tee

El verde es para mí.
el *vair*-deh ess *pa*ra mee

El azul es para Pedro.
el ah-*thool* ess *pa*ra *peh*-dro

El morado es para Clara.
el mor*ah*-tho ess *pa*ra clara

¡Es fantástico!
ess fan-*tass*-teeko

¡Qué divertido!
keh deevair-*tee*-tho

¡Aye, no! ¡Adiós, globos!
aye, noh, adee-*oss glo*-boss

¿Se te ha escapado el globo?
seh teh ah esskap-*ah*-tho el *glo*-bo

¡No pasa nada! ¡No llores!
noh *pa*ssa *nah*-tha, noh *yo*ress

¿Tenéis hambre?
teh-*nayss am*breh

Tomad un poco de pastel.
*to*ma toon *po*co deh pas*tel*

¿Tienes sed?
tee-eh-ness sed

Bebe algo.
beh-beh *al*go

Ha sido una fiesta muy bonita.
ah *see*tho *oo*na fee*ess*ta mwee bo*nee*ta

¡Mirad! ¡Los globos!
*mee*rat, loss *glo*-boss

¡Adiós!
adee-*oss*